W9-AQV-611

Date: 8/29/12

J 597.95 BJO
Bjorklund, Ruth.
Komodo dragons /

KOMODO DRAGONS

by Ruth Bjorklund

Children's Press®

An Imprint of Scholastic Inc.
New York Toronto London Auckland Sydney
Mexico City New Delhi Hong Kong
Danbury, Connecticut

Content Consultant
Dr. Stephen S. Ditchkoff
Professor of Wildlife Sciences
Auburn University
Auburn, Alabama

Photographs © 2012: age fotostock: 1, 2 foreground, 3 foreground,
19, 40 (Reinhard Dirscherl), 32 (SuperStock); Bob Italiano: 44
foreground, 45 foreground; Dreamstime: cover (Daniel Budiman),
15 (Kira Kaplinski), 2 background, 3 background, 44 background,
45 background (Krzysztof Wasilewski), 5 bottom, 8 (Steve Wilson);
Minden Pictures/Michael Pitts/npl: 24, 27; Photo Researchers: 28
(Fletcher & Baylis), 16 (Sylvain Cordier/Biosphoto); Shutterstock, Inc.:
5 top, 36 (Dean Bertoncelj), 11 (Donald Gargano), 4, 5 background,
12 (javarman); Superstock, Inc.: 31, 39 (imagebroker.net), 20, 23,
35 (Minden Pictures), 7 (Woodfall Wild Images/Photoshot/NHPA).

Library of Congress Cataloging-in-Publication Data
Bjorklund, Ruth.
  Komodo dragons/by Ruth Bjorklund.
    p. cm.—(Nature's children)
  Includes bibliographical references and index.
  ISBN-13: 978-0-531-20902-8 (lib. bdg.)
    ISBN-10: 0-531-20902-4 (lib. bdg.)
  ISBN-13: 978-0-531-21077-2 (pbk.)
    ISBN-10: 0-531-21077-4 (pbk.)
  1. Komodo dragon—Juvenile literature. I. Title. II. Series.
  QL666.L29B56 2012
  597.95'968—dc23   2011031129

Printed in China 62
SCHOLASTIC, CHILDREN'S PRESS, and associated logos are
trademarks and/or registered trademarks of Scholastic Inc.

1 2 3 4 5 6 7 8 9 10 R 21 20 19 18 17 16 15 14 13 12

Komodo Dragons

Class	Reptilia
Order	Squamata
Family	Varanidae
Genus	*Varanus*
Species	*komodoensis*
World distribution	Indonesian islands of Komodo, Rinca, Flores, and Gila Motang
Habitats	Hot, dry grasslands; tropical forests
Distinctive physical characteristics	Long tail; bumpy skin made up of bony scales; loose skin around neck; sharp claws and serrated teeth; forked tongue; adults are gray with reddish-brown spots; juveniles are black with red circles on body and yellow, green, and white bands around neck
Habits	Moves around home range alone; ambushes prey and attacks with teeth; poisons victim with powerful bacteria; can eat up to 80 percent of its weight at one time; sleeps in burrows, holes, and caves; males fight each other to breed with females
Diet	Adults eat deer, goats, wild pigs, water buffalo, monkeys, fish, carrion, and younger komodo dragons; juveniles eat insects, birds, and smaller lizards

Contents

CHAPTER 1

Large Lizards

Komodo dragons are the world's largest living lizards. They can reach lengths of 6 to 10 feet (2 to 3 meters) and weigh anywhere from 150 to 300 pounds (68 to 136 kilograms). They live on four small islands in the country of Indonesia. They are found nowhere else in the world.

Komodo dragons sway slowly from side to side as they walk. They walk about 3 miles (4.8 kilometers) per hour and can run as fast as 11 miles (18 km) per hour in short spurts. They are strong swimmers and can dive underwater. Komodo dragons have been known to swim as far as 0.25 miles (402 m) in rough ocean water.

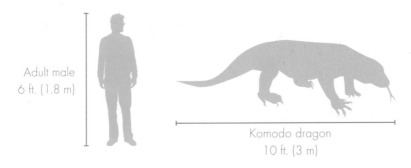

Adult male
6 ft. (1.8 m)

Komodo dragon
10 ft. (3 m)

Komodo dragons have fascinated people around the world for a very long time.

Teeth and Claws

Komodo dragons have long, flat heads. They also have large, powerful tails and strong legs. Bumpy, bony scales cover their bodies and protect them from harm. Sharp claws and serrated teeth help them hunt and kill prey.

The komodo dragon's bite is poisonous. The gums around its teeth are full of slimy mucus and bacteria. The bacteria get into the wound when the komodo dragon bites its prey. This causes an infection that kills the prey.

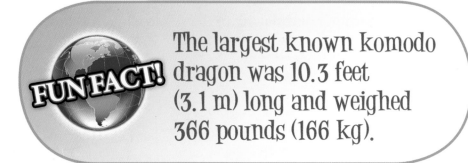

FUN FACT! The largest known komodo dragon was 10.3 feet (3.1 m) long and weighed 366 pounds (166 kg).

Scientists have discovered at least seven different types of poisonous bacteria living in the mouths of komodo dragons.

Cold-Blooded

Komodo dragons live near the equator. The islands they live on are surrounded by the Pacific and Indian Oceans. The average temperature there is about 80 degrees Fahrenheit (27 degrees Celsius) most of the year. But it can soar as high as 110°F (43°C) at times.

These temperature changes have a big effect on komodo dragons. They are cold-blooded. This means they do not have steady inner temperatures. Their body temperatures fall when it is cold outside and rise when it is hot. The inner body temperature of a komodo dragon matches the temperature of the air. Komodo dragons control their temperatures by basking on warm rocks during colder weather and staying in the shade when it is hot.

Rocks heat up in the sunlight and help komodo dragons raise their body temperatures.

Different Senses

Smell is a komodo dragon's most powerful sense. But komodo dragons don't smell with their nostrils. Instead, they use tiny sacs in the roof of their mouths called Jacobson's organs. A komodo dragon captures odor **particles** in the air when it flicks out its forked tongue. The particles touch the Jacobson's organ when the lizard pulls its tongue back into its mouth. The Jacobson's organ sends messages to the brain. This helps the komodo dragon hunt prey, search for a **mate**, and find its way in the dark.

Komodo dragons can see color. But their overall vision is poor. They have no taste buds on their tongues and only a few in their throats. Komodo dragons have ear holes on each side of their heads, but they are nearly deaf. They have touch sensors on their faces and the bottoms of their feet that connect to **nerves** in their bodies. These sensors are the only places where komodo dragons have a strong sense of touch. Their thick scales make it difficult to feel much on the rest of their bodies.

Komodo dragons have very long tongues.

CHAPTER 2

How Komodo Dragons Survive

Most Indonesian islands are filled with plant and animal life. But Komodo Island and its neighbors are dry and barren. They do not support much life. The komodo dragon survives because it can go without food or water for long periods of time.

Komodo dragons are top predators. No other animal hunts them or threatens to eat their food. They are carnivores. They usually eat carrion. They also hunt for live animals such as deer, goats, wild pigs, monkeys, and fish. A komodo dragon can attack and kill animals nearly twice its weight.

Komodo dragons spend much of their time foraging for carrion. They only hunt for prey if they do not find any carrion. Then Komodo dragons use their Jacobson's organs to track their prey. They hide and wait. Their dull coloring helps them blend into the rocks and grass.

Komodo dragons will eat any animal they can catch and kill.

The Attack

A komodo dragon uses many different means of attack. Sometimes its prey is high in the trees or up on a rocky ledge. The komodo dragon stands on its back legs and uses its mighty tail for support to reach the animal.

Komodo dragons are patient hunters. They often ambush unsuspecting prey. A komodo dragon can hide for weeks at a time. It pounces when its prey walks past the hiding place. It sinks its sharp teeth into the animal's leg, throat, or belly and shreds it apart. If the injured prey escapes, the komodo dragon simply follows behind it until it dies.

Komodo dragons also eat fish. They wait in the water for island fishers to set their catch on the beach to dry. Then they use their powerful legs to swim to shore and steal the fish!

Komodo dragons can easily reach animals that are in the lower branches of trees.

Big Eaters

Komodo dragons eat as much of their prey as they can. They often eat up to 80 percent of their body weight at once. Komodo dragons eat so much at each meal that they only need to eat about once a month.

Komodo dragons hold their prey with their thick front legs and claws. They use their teeth to tear off large chunks of meat and swallow them whole. They eat every part of the animal, including fur, teeth, and hooves.

Komodo dragons lay in the sun after they are done eating. This helps them warm their bodies and digest their food.

FUN FACT! Komodo dragons' throats stretch so they can swallow huge chunks of prey whole.

Komodo dragons do not let any part of their prey go to waste.

CHAPTER 3

Daily Life

Food is not plentiful on the komodo dragons' home islands. Komodo dragons must cover a wide area to find carrion or prey. A large komodo dragon walks as much as 6 miles (10 km) each day. It can spend more than 20 days in a row searching for each meal. Komodo dragons rarely meet each other except to mate or share a carcass.

The biggest and highest-ranking males eat first if a group of komodo dragons forms around a large piece of carrion. The komodo dragons often fight if they get too close to one another. The larger and stronger dragon will hiss and thrash its tail. It will also stand on its hind legs, arch its back, and puff out the loose skin around its neck. The weaker komodo dragon may be killed and eaten if it does not run off.

About 10 percent of a komodo dragon's diet is made up of other komodo dragons.

Home Sweet Home

Each komodo dragon has its own home range. The home range includes a sleeping area, a carrion foraging area, and hunting grounds. The size of the home range depends on how large and powerful the komodo dragon is.

Komodo dragons sleep alone in burrows. A burrow is a nest dug out of dirt, an opening in a cave, or a hole in rocks or tree roots. Each komodo dragon makes its own burrow. It uses its powerful legs to dig into the ground. Then it backs into the burrow and curls up so that both its head and its tail stick out.

A komodo dragon sleeps about 12 hours a day. It wakes early in the morning. It might spend most of the morning basking in the sun if it is cool outside. Then it forages for carrion.

Burrows are often just large enough for the komodo dragon to fit inside.

Mating

Komodo dragons mate every year between May and October. Male komodo dragons fight each other over females. The winning male then must convince the female to mate with him. Females hiss and claw at males. Males and females often continue to attack each other even after they finish mating.

The female komodo dragon lays her eggs in a burrow or a bird's nest. The group of eggs is called a clutch. There are usually about 20 eggs in a komodo dragon's clutch. The female sits on the eggs to protect them and keep them warm. It takes about eight to nine months for the eggs to hatch.

Hatchling komodo dragons use a special tooth to crack their way out of their eggs. They hatch at the end of the islands' rainy season. This means there are many insects for the newborn komodo dragons to eat.

Baby komodo dragons are about 15 inches (38 centimeters) long when they hatch.

Growing Up

Young komodo dragons have a hard life. They are weak and helpless after hatching. Their mothers do not take care of them. They are left to fend for themselves. Komodo dragons are cannibals. Older komodo dragons often dig babies out of their nests and eat them.

After hatching and leaving their nests, young komodo dragons seek safety from predators by living in trees. The young komodo dragons eat insects, birds, eggs, and smaller lizards while living in the trees. They become juveniles after about a year.

The juveniles leave the trees and begin eating carrion after a few years. Juveniles are not as powerful as older komodo dragons. This means they only eat after all of the older komodo dragons have eaten. Juveniles are in danger of attacks from adults until they are about five or six years old. Juveniles roll in feces and the rotting guts of carrion to discourage adults from eating them.

Young komodo dragons make meals of the small beetles and geckos they find in the treetops.

CHAPTER 4

The History of the Komodo Dragon

Lizards lived during the time of the dinosaurs. The dinosaurs died out around 65 million years ago. Nearly 70 percent of all the other species on Earth died along with them. Lizards were among the animals that survived.

Komodo dragons belong to the genus *Varanus*. Fossil remains of other *Varanus* animals date back more than 34 million years. The word *Varanus* comes from an Arabic word for "monitor."

Ancient monitor lizards lived in Australia and Asia. These two continents were closer together about 2 million years ago than they are today. The sea level was also lower. Komodo dragons were able to migrate to the islands where they live today.

Scientists learn about komodo dragon ancestors by studying their fossilized remains.

Discovery

Komodo dragons were once known only on their home islands. They were hidden from the rest of the world, although local people told rumors about a mysterious "land crocodile." In the early 20th century, Indonesian pearl divers claimed they had seen a dragon. They reported this information to the Indonesian government.

The director of an Indonesian zoological museum sent hunters to Komodo Island in 1912. He ordered them to find and bring back the "dragon." The hunters killed two adult komodo dragons and returned with their bodies. They also captured and brought along two live baby komodo dragons. The zoo director realized that the animal was not a dragon. It was a giant monitor lizard. He gave it the scientific name *Varanus komodoensis*.

Komodo dragons are a common sight along the coasts of their home islands.

Hunters on Komodo Island

An American adventurer named Douglas Burden heard about the giant lizard a few years later. The American Museum of Natural History sent him on an expedition to Indonesia. Burden sailed 15,000 miles (24,000 km) aboard the SS *Dog* and landed on Komodo Island in 1926. He brought his wife, a big game hunter, a scientist, and others. The group killed 12 adult komodo dragons. They brought them back to America along with two live specimens.

Word spread about the discovery. Private collectors and zoos around the world hoped to get komodo dragons of their own. Hunters began killing and capturing large numbers of komodo dragons to meet the demand.

In 1938, the Indonesian government made it illegal to hunt komodo dragons on Komodo Island. Only a team of scientists was allowed near the komodo dragons. Scientists lived among the lizards for 11 months in 1969. They carefully studied how komodo dragons lived.

Komodo dragons are a popular attraction at many zoos around the world.

CHAPTER 5

Komodo Dragons Today

Many animal protection groups have komodo dragons on their threatened and endangered species lists. This means that they are in danger of becoming extinct. Komodo dragons and other endangered species will need help surviving into the future.

Komodo dragons are powerful animals. But they still face many obstacles in their struggle to survive. Humans cause some of these obstacles. Others are simply a result of natural disasters. Komodo Island and the other islands where komodo dragons live are harsh. Volcanoes, wildfires, and earthquakes have all been known to occur there. These and other disasters can quickly kill large numbers of komodo dragons.

Scientists must be very careful to avoid injury while studying wild komodo dragons.

Natural Disasters

The balance of nature on Komodo and nearby islands is delicate. Natural disasters can easily throw this balance off. This makes it very hard for plants and animals on the islands to recover. In the 1980s, a wildfire burned most of the plants on the island of Padar. Plant-eating animals died because of a lack of food. Komodo dragons on Padar had relied on these plant-eating animals for prey. Padar's komodo dragon population soon disappeared because of the lack of food. There are no komodo dragons left on Padar today.

Padar is not the only island to experience natural disasters. Nearby volcanoes sometimes erupt and spread ash over the other islands where komodo dragons live. This kills plants and has an effect similar to that of the Padar wildfire. After an earthquake in 1992, a massive tsunami wiped out many of the plants and animals on the island of Flores. The komodo dragon population on Flores remains very small because of this tsunami.

A Komodo dragon can be shades of blue and red in changing light conditions.

Human Invasion

Komodo dragons share their island homes with many small villages. Villagers live simply by farming and fishing. But they cut trees to build houses and clear the land for farming. They also try to keep the dangerous komodo dragons away from their villages. Some use poisoned carrion to kill komodo dragons.

Logging companies cut down areas of forest. This destroys the komodo dragons' habitat. These activities can upset the balance of nature and hurt the animal population.

Hunters are another huge threat to komodo dragons. Some hunt by setting wildfires to scare animals out of the forests. Poachers kill large numbers of deer. This leaves less food for komodo dragons. Poachers also capture komodo dragons to sell to collectors. Other people kill komodo dragons for their skins.

Komodo dragons are an unwelcome sight in towns and villages.

Komodo National Park

Indonesia is proud to be the home of such a rare and interesting species. The Indonesian government established Komodo National Park in 1980. The park covers Komodo, Rinca, and Gila Motang. It does not include Flores because there are so few komodo dragons there. The park protects thousands of komodo dragons. It has strict laws against poaching. Park rangers teach local children about protecting their environment to save komodo dragons and other species. Tourists visit from around the world. Their money keeps the park running. It also creates jobs for villagers.

Zoos in places such as Australia and Hawaii raise komodo dragons. But it is more important that komodo dragons survive in the wild. Like all plant and animal species, they play an important role in the natural world.

Park rangers protect and control the komodo dragon population at Komodo National Park.

Words to Know

ambush (AM-bush) — to attack from a hiding place

bacteria (bak-TEER-ee-uh) — microscopic, single-celled living things that exist everywhere and can be either useful or harmful

barren (BAR-uhn) — unable to support plant life

basking (BASK-ing) — lying or sitting in the sun

cannibals (KAN-uh-buhlz) — animals that eat other animals of their own kind

carnivores (KAR-nih-vorz) — animals that have meat as a regular part of their diet

carrion (KAR-ee-uhn) — dead animal flesh

clutch (KLUHCH) — a nest of eggs

endangered (en-DAYN-jurd) — at risk of becoming extinct, usually because of human activity

equator (i-KWAY-tur) — an imaginary line around the middle of Earth that is an equal distance from the North and South Poles

extinct (ik-STINGKT) — no longer found alive

foraging (FOR-ij-ing) — searching for food

genus (JEE-nuhs) — a group of related plants or animals that is larger than a species but smaller than a family

habitat (HAB-uh-tat) — the place where an animal or a plant is usually found

juveniles (JOO-vuh-nuhlz) — animals that are neither babies nor adults

mate (MAYT) — an animal that joins with another animal to reproduce

migrate (MY-grayt) — to move from one area to another

nerves (NURVZ) — the threads that send messages between the brain and other parts of the body to move and feel

particles (PAHR-ti-kuhlz) — extremely small pieces or amounts of something

poachers (POH-churz) — people who hunt or fish illegally

prey (PRAY) — an animal that's hunted by another animal for food

serrated (SEHR-a-ted) — having a jagged edge

species (SPEE-sheez) — one of the groups into which animals and plants of the same genus are divided

specimens (SPES-uh-muhnz) — samples used to stand for a whole group

threatened (THRET-uhnd) — at risk of becoming endangered

tsunami (tsoo-NAH-mee) — a very large, destructive wave caused by an underwater earthquake or volcano

NORTH

AMERICA

PACIFIC

OCEAN

ATLANTIC

SOUTH
AMERICA

Komodo Dragon Range

ARCTIC OCEAN

EUROPE

ASIA

AFRICA

PACIFIC
OCEAN

INDIAN
OCEAN

OCEAN

AUSTRALIA

Komodo

Flores

Rinca

Find Out More

Books

Kalman, Bobbie. *Endangered Komodo Dragons*. New York: Crabtree Publishers, 2005.

Marsico, Katie. *A Komodo Hatchling Grows Up*. New York: Children's Press, 2007.

O'Donnell, Kerri. *Komodo Dragons*. New York: PowerKids Press, 2007.

Web Sites

American Museum of Natural History—Komodo Dragon
www.amnh.org/nationalcenter/Endangered/ora/ora.html
Learn more about komodo dragons.

Animal Planet—Komodo Dragon
http://animal.discovery.com/reptiles/komodo-dragon/
Check out photos and videos of komodo dragons.

Honolulu Zoo—Komodo Dragon
www.honoluluzoo.org/komodo_dragon.htm
Find out how one zoo is working to raise komodo dragons in captivity.

Visit this Scholastic web site for more information on komodo dragons:
www.factsfornow.scholastic.com

Index

About the Author

Ruth Bjorklund lives on an island near Seattle, Washington. She is a former children's librarian and has written numerous books for children and teens, including a guide about raising lizards as pets. She has traveled to Indonesia and regrets not visiting Komodo National Park.